EASY PIANO
THE BEST OF ANDREW LLOYD W
ARRANGED BY BILL BOYD

T0048389

The public performance of any of the works contained in this edition in a dramatic form or context is expressly prohibited.

ISBN 978-0-7935-0603-3

7777 W. BLUEMOUND RD. P.O. BOX 13819 MILWAUKEE, WI 53213

EASY PIANO
THE BEST OF ANDREW LLOYD WEBBER
ARRANGED BY BILL BOYD

CONTENTS

ALL I ASK OF YOU
(From "THE PHANTOM OF THE OPERA")

Music by ANDREW LLOYD WEBBER
Lyrics by CHARLES HART
Additional Lyrics by RICHARD STILGOE

Slowly (in two)

RAOUL:

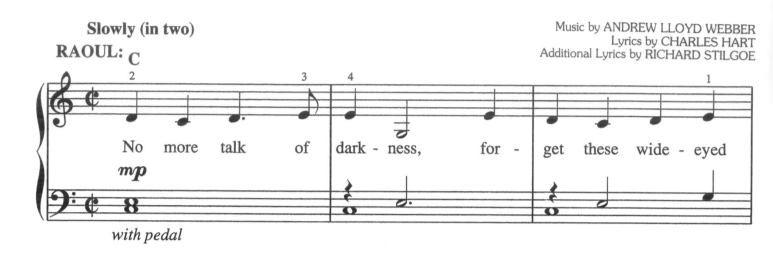

with pedal

No more talk of dark-ness, for-get these wide-eyed

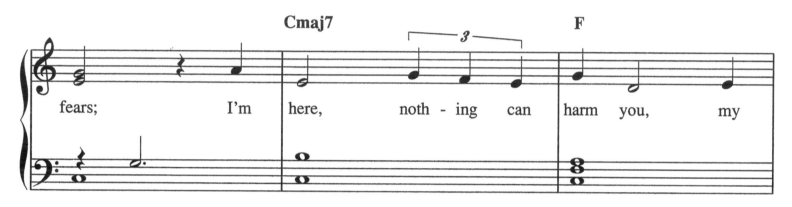

fears; I'm here, noth-ing can harm you, my

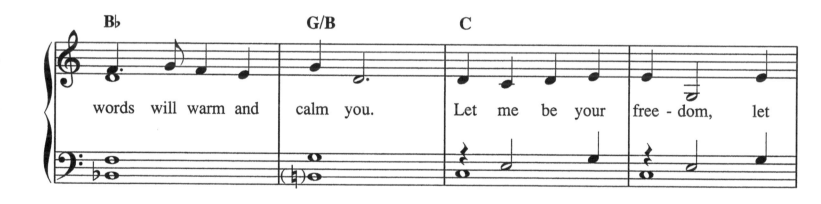

words will warm and calm you. Let me be your free-dom, let

day-light dry your tears; I'm here, with you, be-

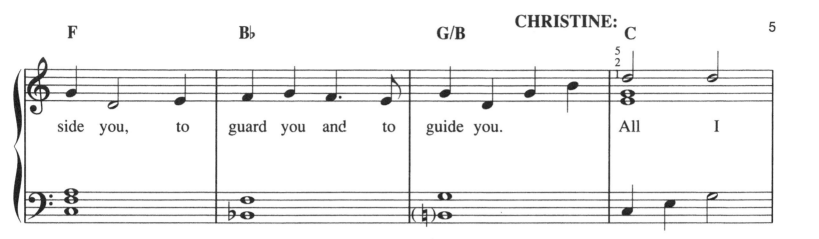

side you, to guard you and to guide you. All I

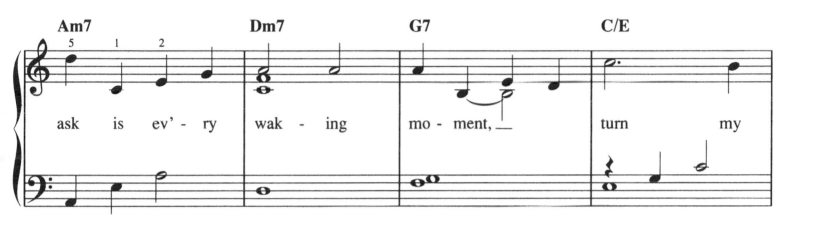

ask is ev'-ry wak - ing mo - ment, __ turn my

head with talk of sum - mer-time.

Say you need me with you now and al - ways; __

6

C/E   F   C/E   G

pro - mise me that all you say is true, that's all I ask of

rit.

RAOUL:

C

mf
Let me be your shel - ter, let me be your light; you're
you.

a tempo

Cmaj7   3   F   B♭

safe, no one will find you, your fears are far be -

CHRISTINE:

G/B   C

hind you. All I want is free - dom, a world with no more

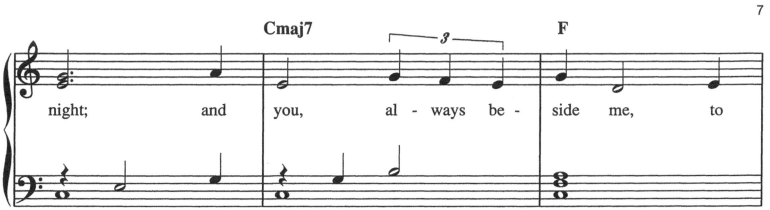

night;   and   you,   al - ways be -   side   me,   to

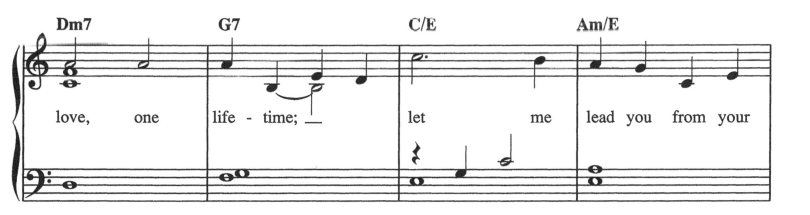

RAOUL:

hold   me   and   to   hide   me.   Then   say   you'll   share   with   me   one

love,   one   life - time; ___   let   me   lead   you   from   your

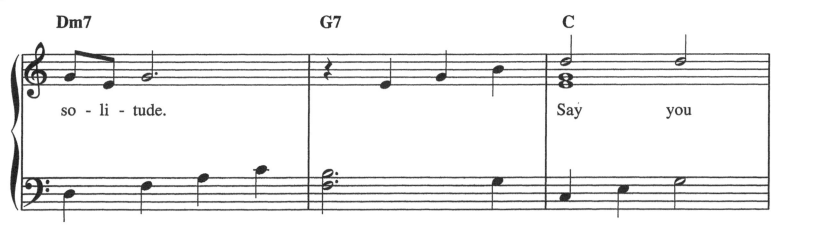

so - li - tude.   Say   you

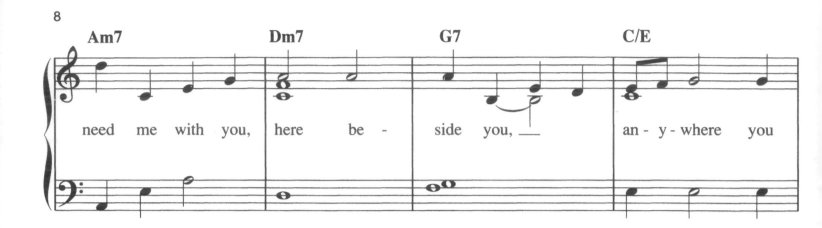

need me with you, here be - side you, ___ an - y - where you

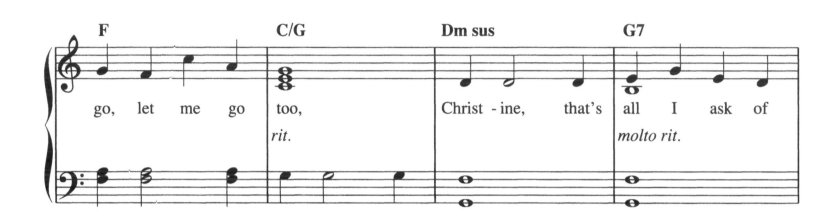

go, let me go too, Christ - ine, that's all I ask of

rit. *molto rit.*

CHRISTINE:

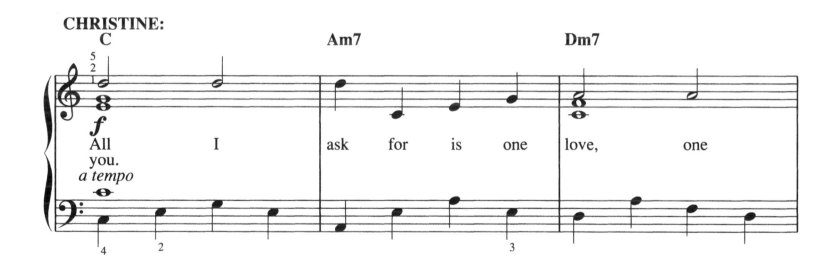

All I ask for is one love, one

you.

a tempo

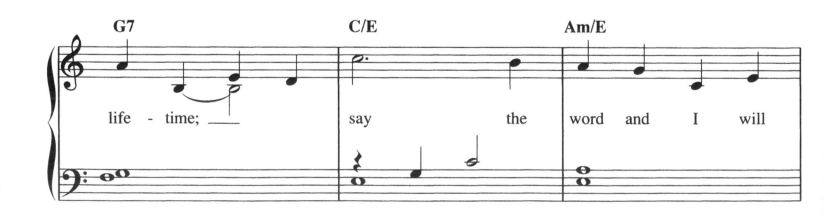

life - time; ___ say the word and I will

TOGETHER:

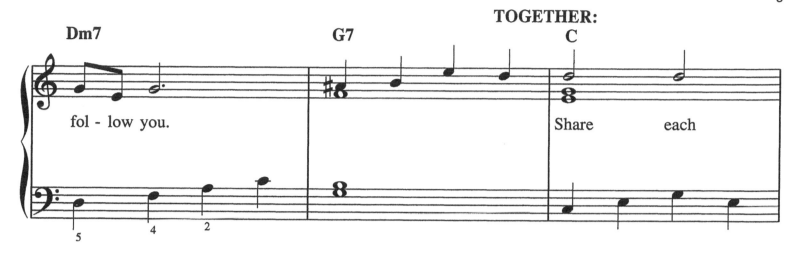

fol - low you.

Share each

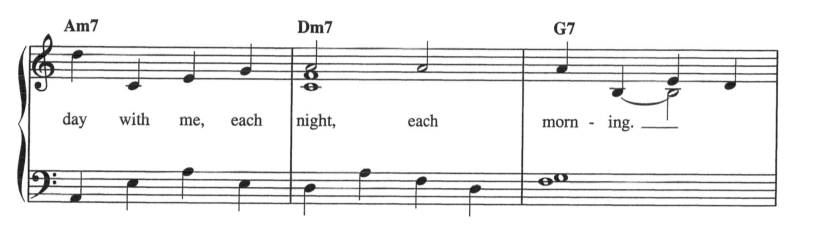

day with me, each night, each morn - ing. _____

Slower

An - y - where you go, let me go too;

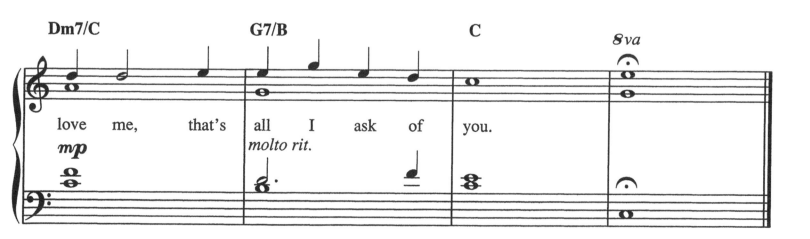

love me, that's all I ask of you.

molto rit.

DON'T CRY FOR ME ARGENTINA

(From The Opera "EVITA")

Lyric by TIM RICE
Music by ANDREW LLOYD WEBBER

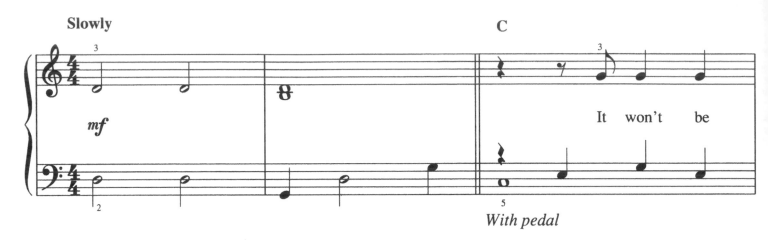

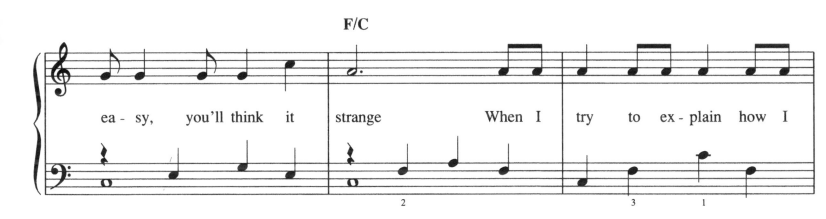

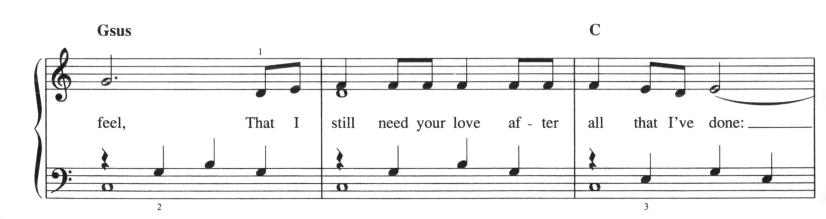

MCA music publishing

You won't be - lieve me   All you will see is a

girl you once knew   Al - though she's dressed up to the nines   at

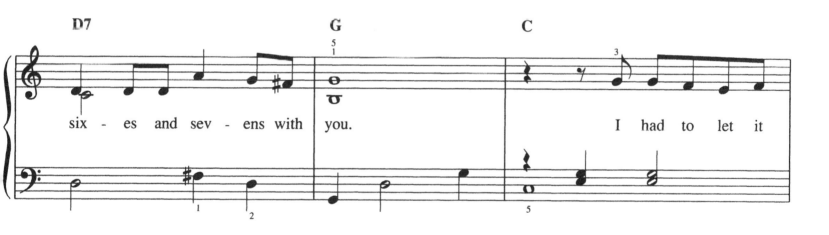

six - es and sev - ens with you.   I had to let it

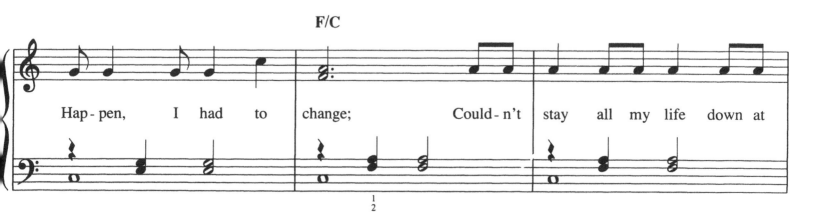

Hap - pen, I had to change;   Could - n't stay all my life down at

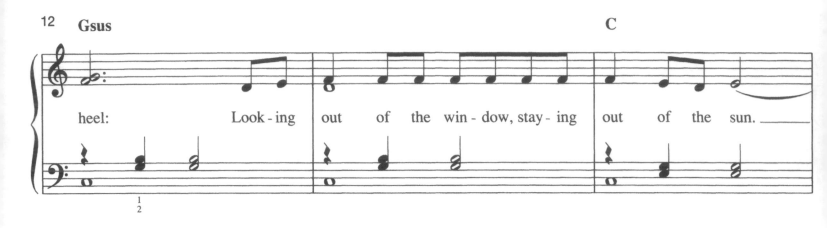

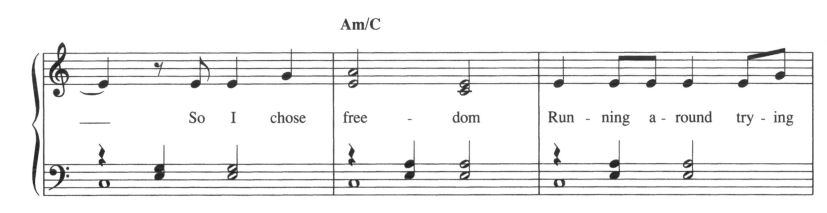

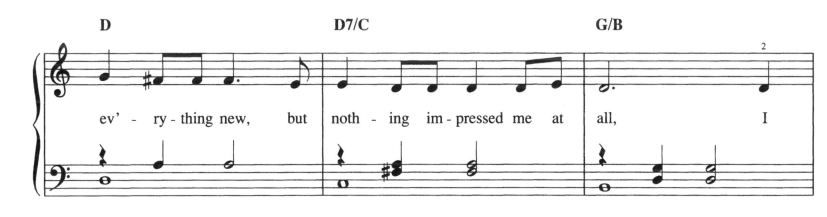

ti - na____ the truth is I nev - er left you: All through my wild days, my mad ex-

ist - ence, I kept my prom - ise don't keep your dis - tance.____ Don't cry for me Ar - gen-

ti - na____ the truth is I nev - er left you: All through my wild days, my mad ex-

ist - ence I kept my prom - ise *rit.* don't keep your dis - tance.____

I DON'T KNOW HOW TO LOVE HIM

(From "JESUS CHRIST SUPERSTAR")

Words by TIM RICE
Music by ANDREW LLOYD WEBBER

Slowly and tenderly

mp I don't know how to love _____ him What to do, how to

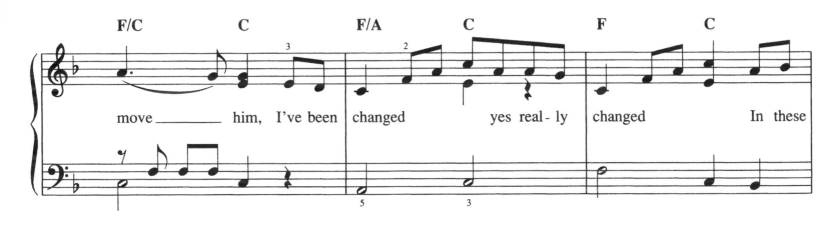

move _____ him, I've been changed yes real-ly changed In these

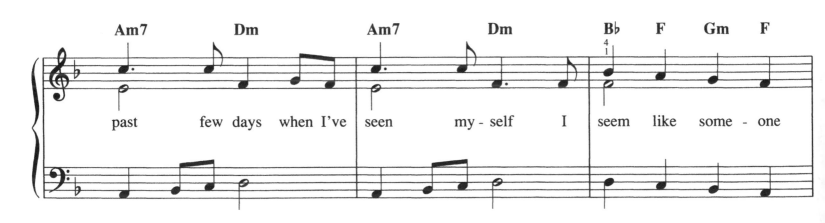

past few days when I've seen my-self I seem like some-one

MCA music publishing

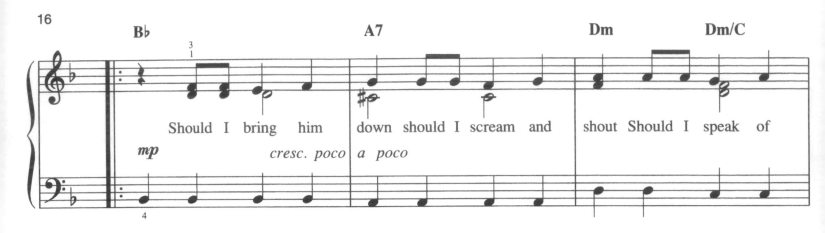

Should I bring him down should I scream and shout Should I speak of

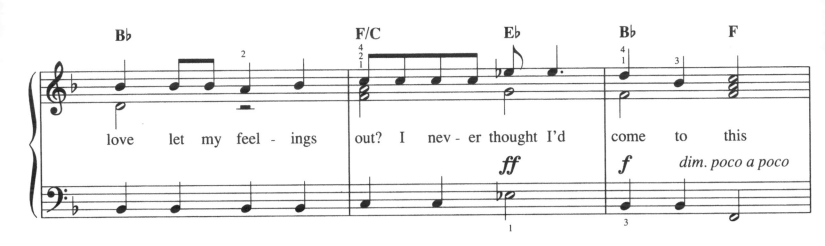

love let my feel-ings out? I nev-er thought I'd come to this

what's it all a - bout?

Don't you think it's rath-er fun - ny I should be in this po-
Yet if he said he loved _____ me I'd be lost I'd be

si - tion? I'm the one who's al - ways been So
fright - ened I could-n't cope just could-n't cope I'd

calm so cool no lov-er's fool Run - ning ev' - ry___
turn my head I'd back a - way I would - n't want to___

1.
show He scares me so
know He scares me

2.
so I want him

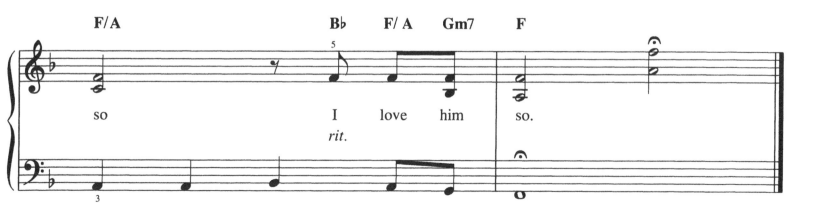

F/A

so
rit.

Bb F/A Gm7 F

I love him so.

MR. MISTOFFELEES

(From "CATS")

Music by ANDREW LLOYD WEBBER
Text by T.S. ELIOT

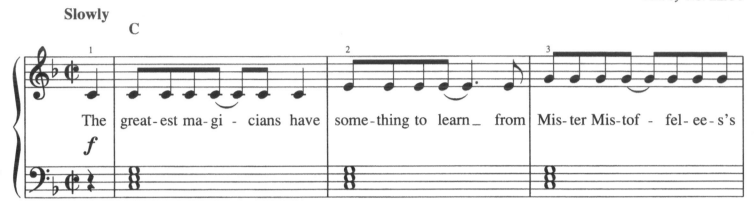

The great-est ma-gi - cians have some-thing to learn _ from Mis-ter Mis-tof - fel-ee-s's

Con-jur-ing Turn._ Pre-sto! And we all say, Oh Well I

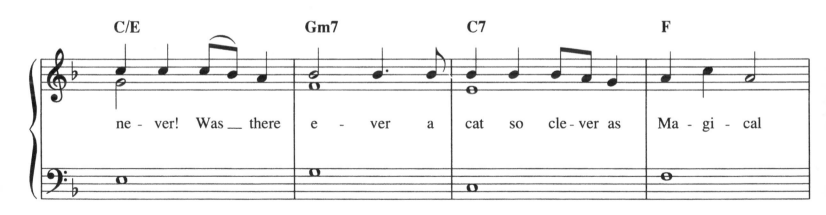

ne - ver! Was _ there e - ver a cat so cle-ver as Ma - gi - cal

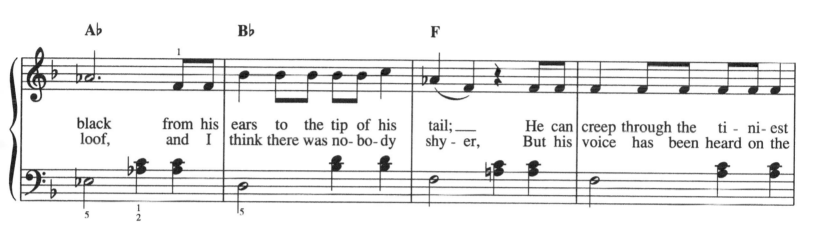

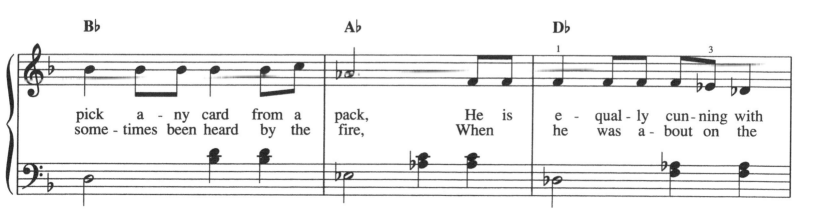

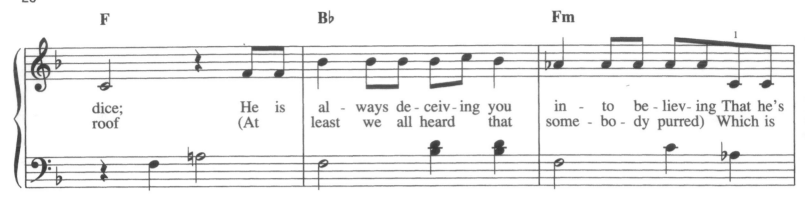

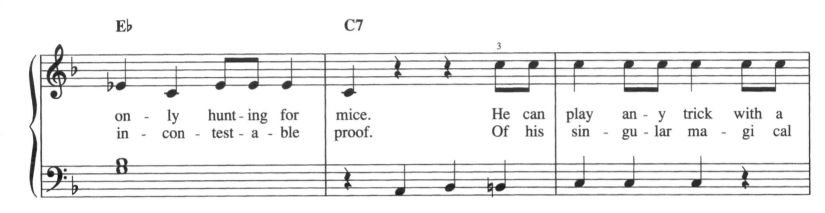

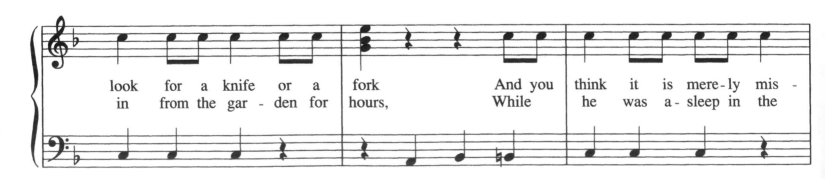

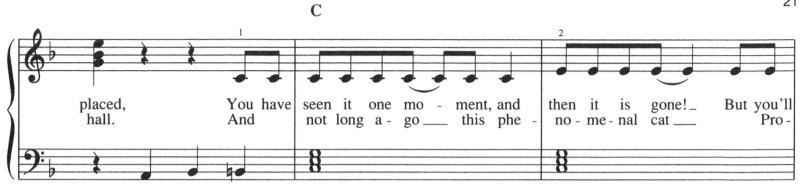

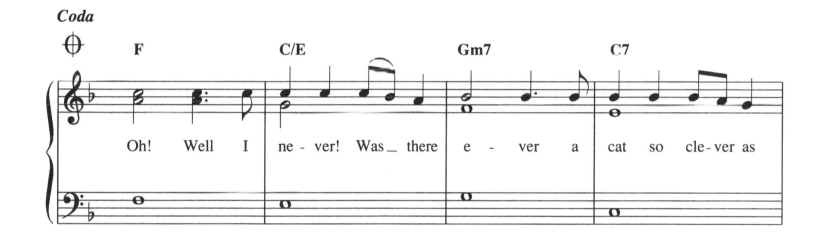

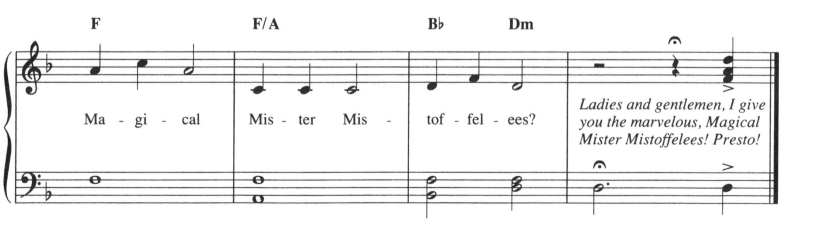

MEMORY
(From "CATS")

Music by ANDREW LLOYD WEBBER
Text by TREVOR NUNN after T.S. ELIOT

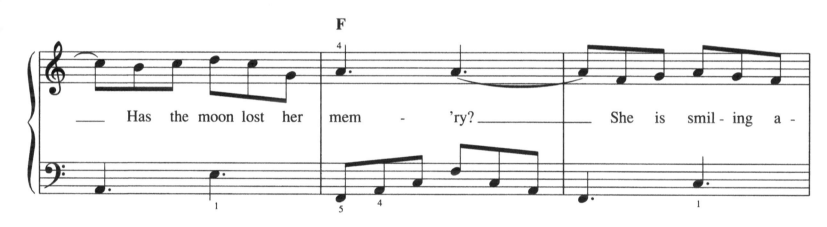

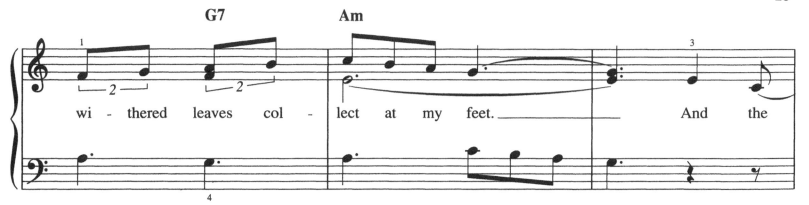

wi - thered leaves col - lect at my feet._____ And the

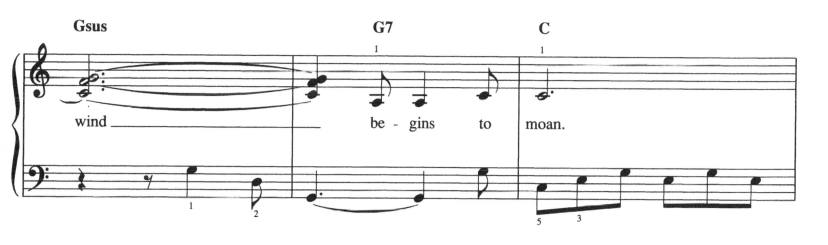

wind _____ be - gins to moan.

Mem - 'ry _____ all a - lone in the moon - light. _____

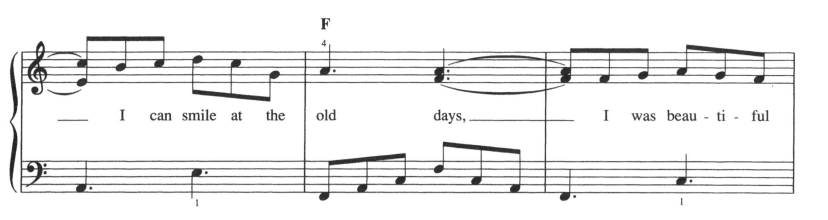

_____ I can smile at the old days,_____ I was beau - ti - ful

then, _____ I re - mem - ber the

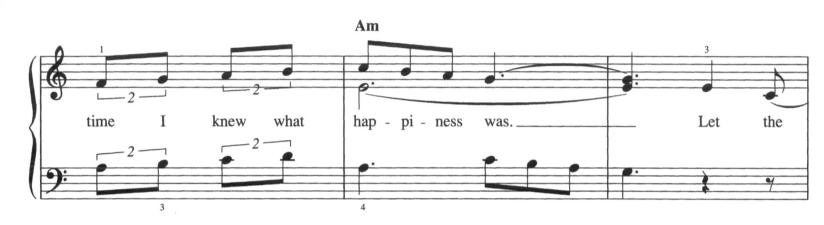

time I knew what hap - pi - ness was. _____ Let the

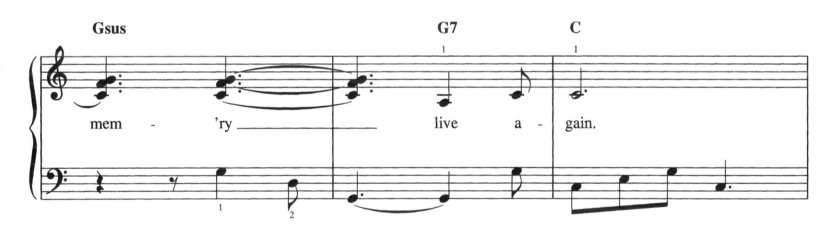

mem - 'ry _____ live a - gain.

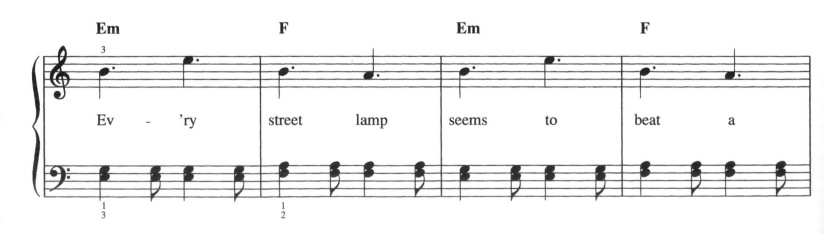

Ev - 'ry street lamp seems to beat a

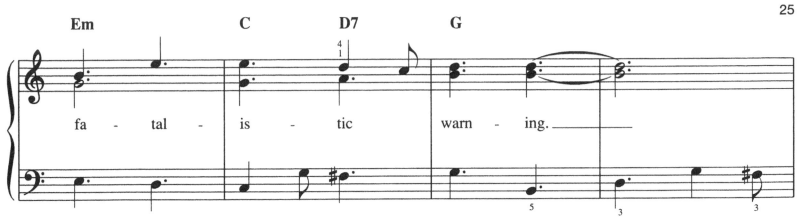

fa - tal - is - tic warn - ing.

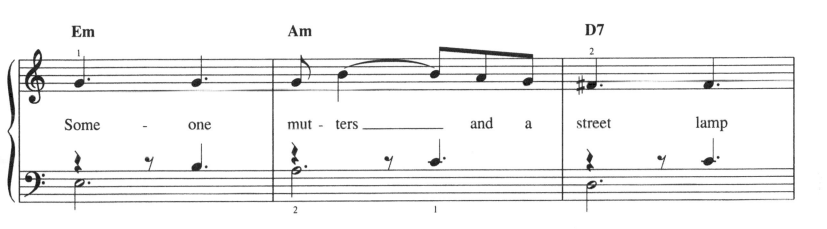

Some - one mut - ters _____ and a street lamp

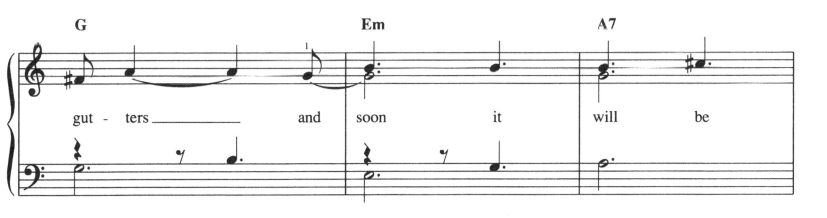

gut - ters _____ and soon it will be

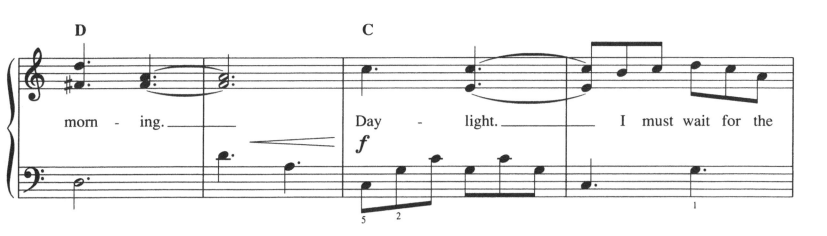

morn - ing. _____ Day - light. _____ I must wait for the

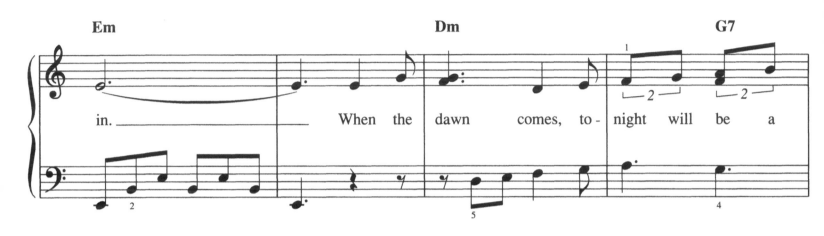

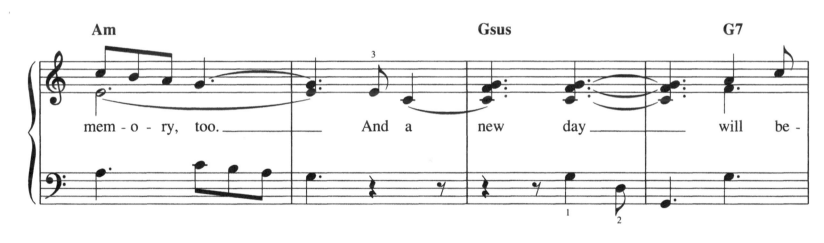

THE MUSIC OF THE NIGHT
(From "THE PHANTOM OF THE OPERA")

Music by ANDREW LLOYD WEBBER
Lyrics by CHARLES HART
Additional Lyrics by RICHARD STILGOE

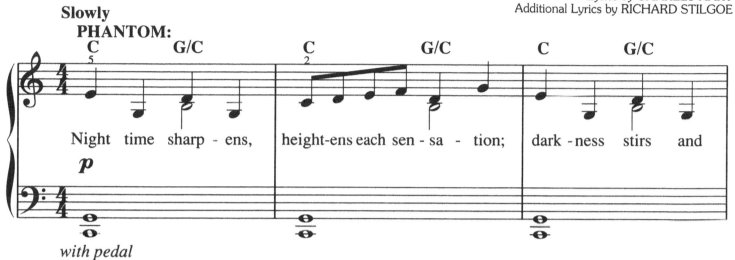

Night time sharp-ens, height-ens each sen-sa-tion; dark-ness stirs and

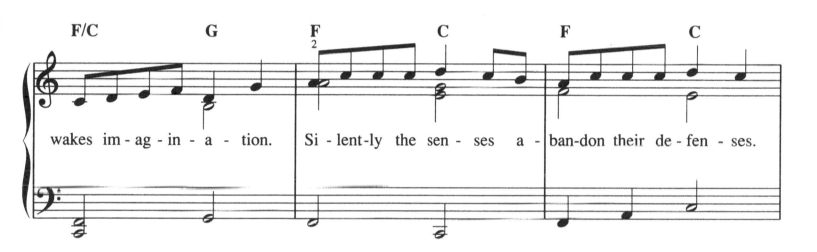

wakes im-ag-in-a-tion. Si-lent-ly the sen-ses a-ban-don their de-fen-ses.

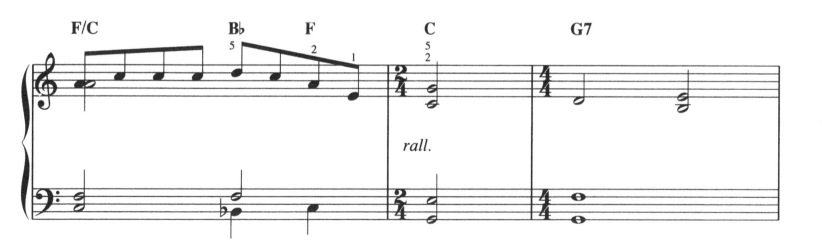

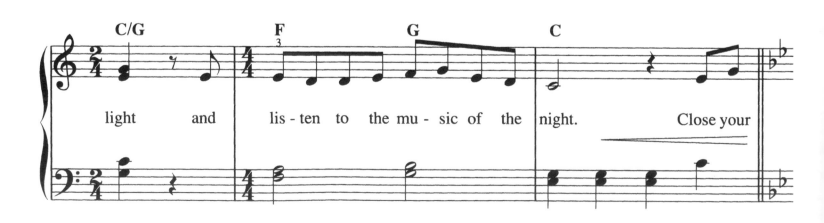

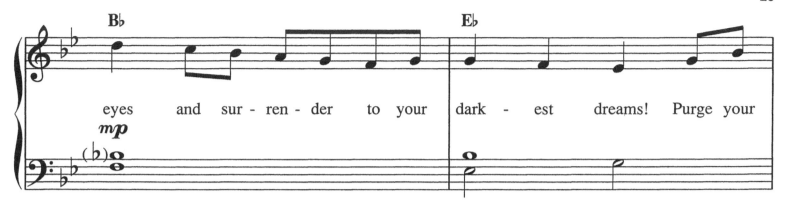

eyes   and sur - ren - der to your dark - est dreams! Purge your

thoughts   of   the life you knew be - fore!   Close your

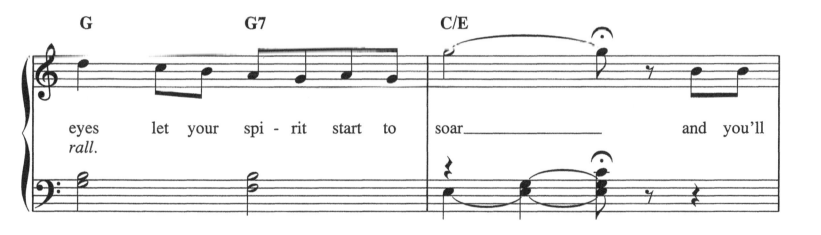

eyes   let your spi - rit start to   soar_____ and you'll
rall.

live   as you've nev - er lived be - fore.   Soft - ly,   deft - ly,
rit.   *a tempo*

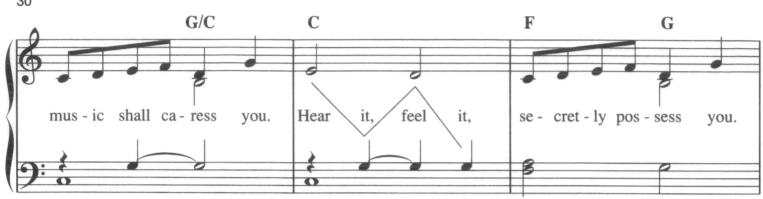

mus - ic shall ca - ress you. Hear it, feel it, se - cret - ly pos - sess you.

O - pen up your mind, let your fan - ta - sies un - wind in this

dark-ness which you know you can-not fight, the dark-ness of the mu - sic of the

night. Let your mind start a jour - ney through a

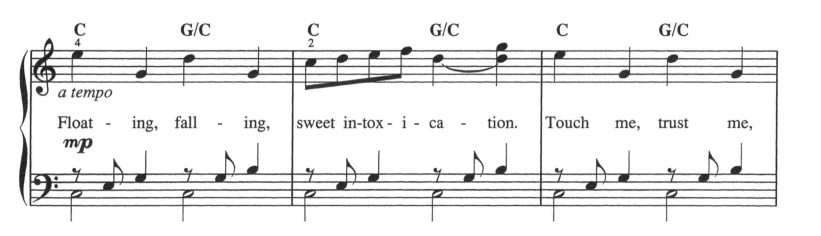

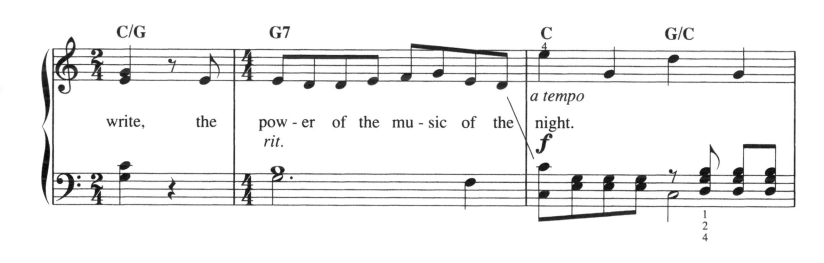

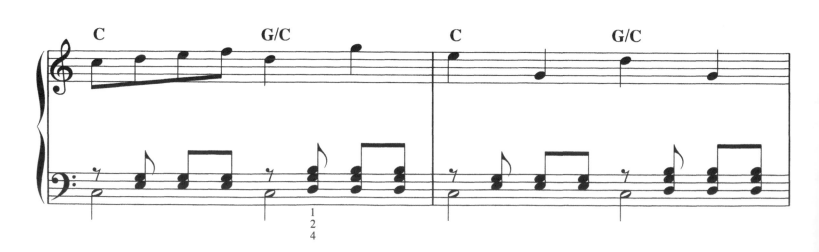

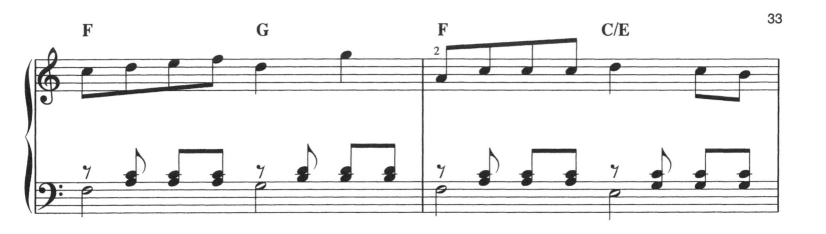

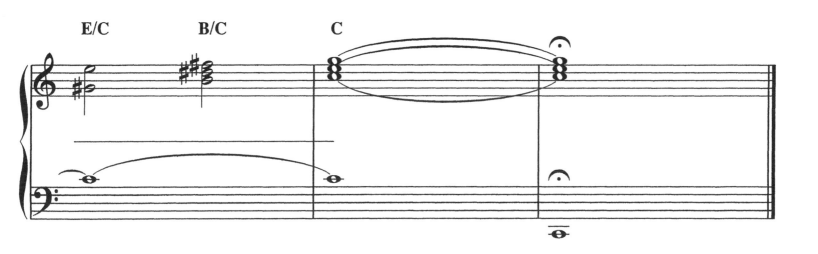

THE PHANTOM OF THE OPERA
(From "THE PHANTOM OF THE OPERA")

Music by ANDREW LLOYD WEBBER
Lyrics by CHARLES HART
Additional Lyrics by RICHARD STILGOE and MIKE BATT

Moderately fast

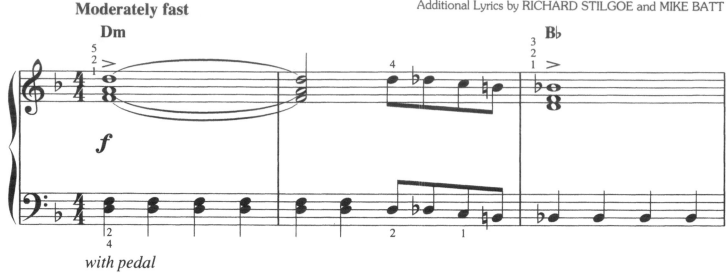

with pedal

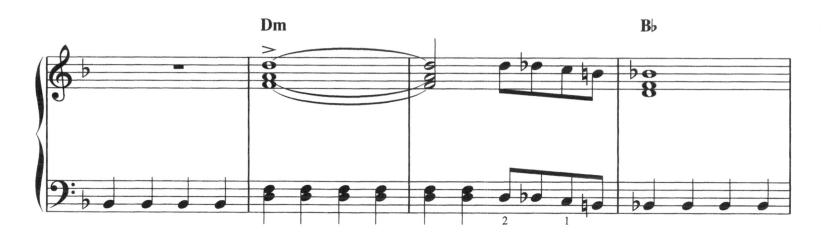

CHRISTINE:

In sleep he

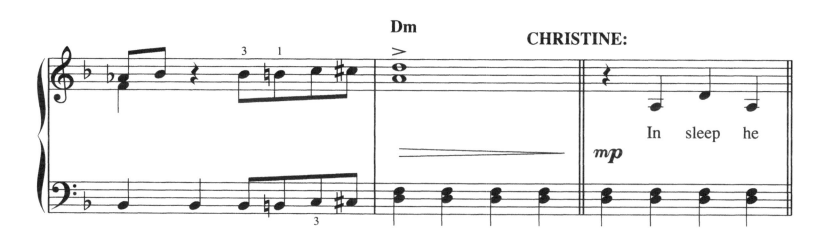

sang to me, _____ in dreams he came, that voice which

calls to me _____ and speaks my name. And do I

dream a - gain? _____ For now I find _____ the

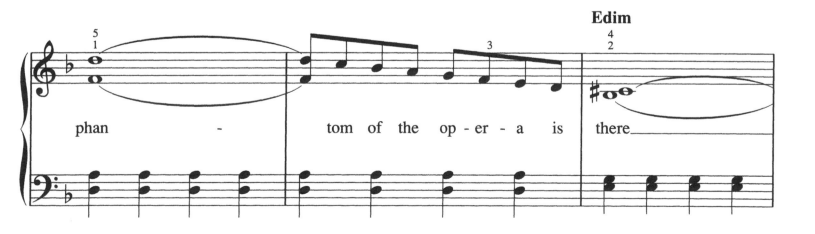

phan - tom of the op - er - a is there _____

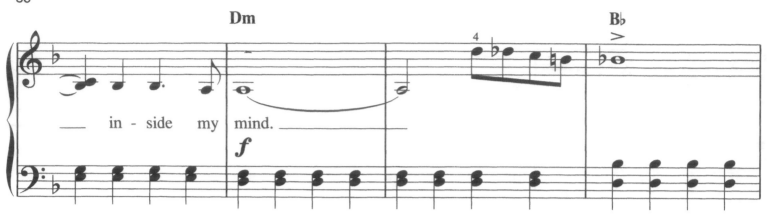

in - side my mind.

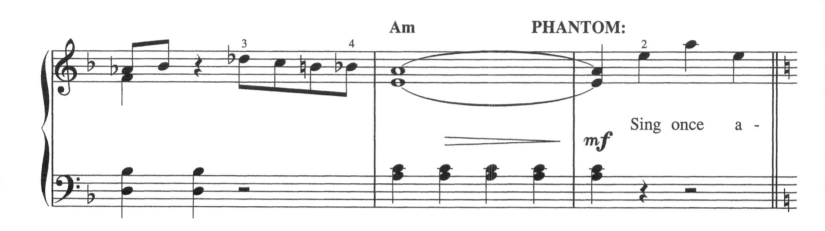

PHANTOM:

Sing once a -

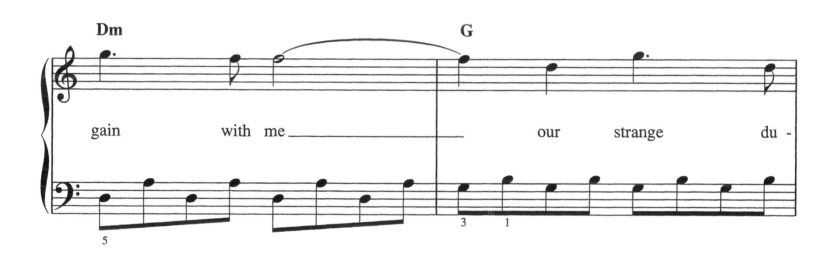

gain with me   our strange du -

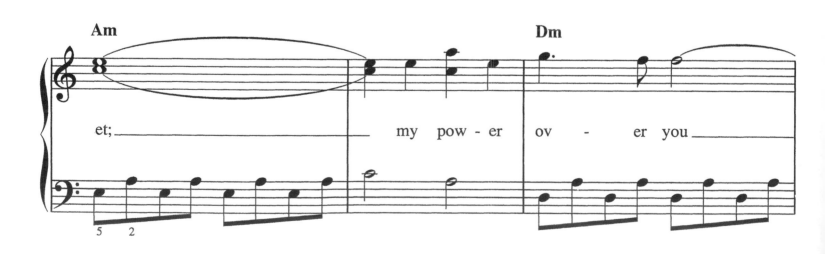

et;   my pow - er ov - er you

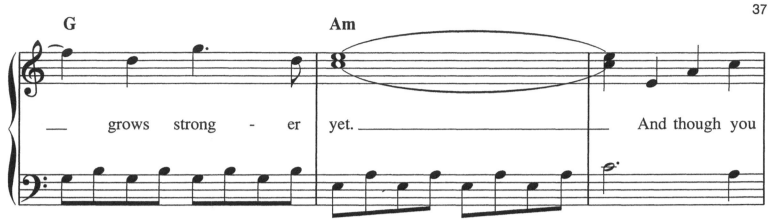

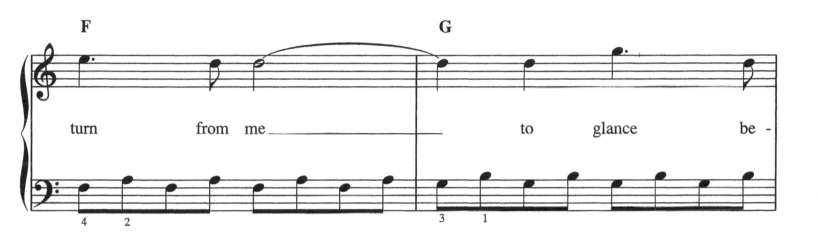

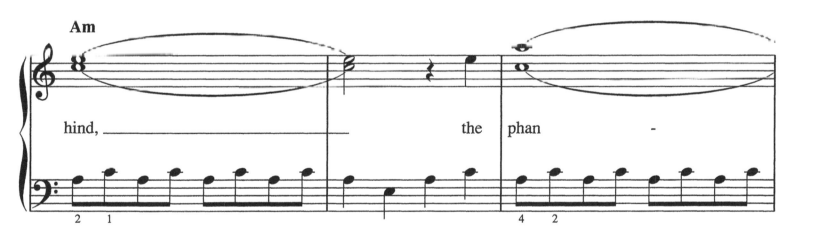

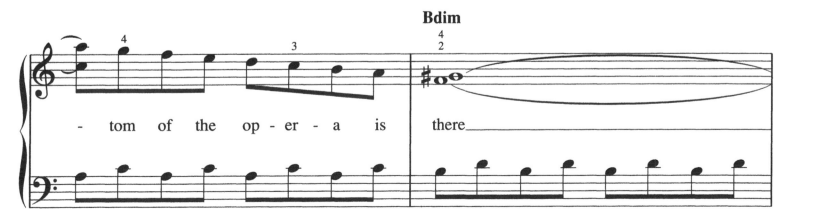

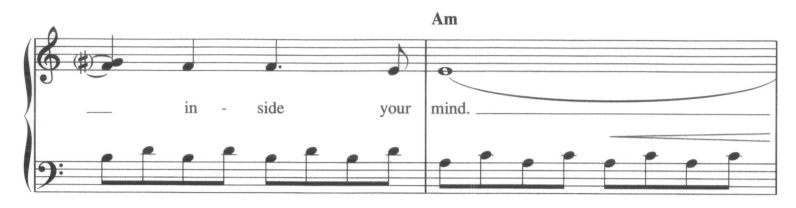

in - side your mind. _____

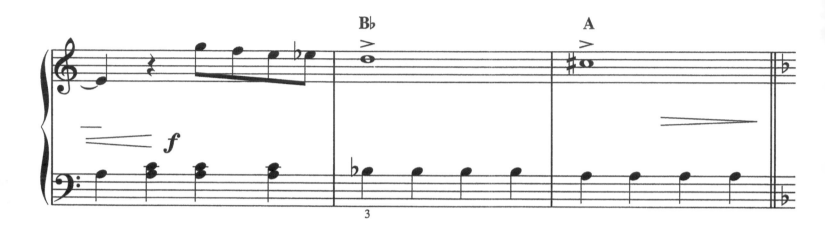

CHRISTINE:

Those who have seen your face _____

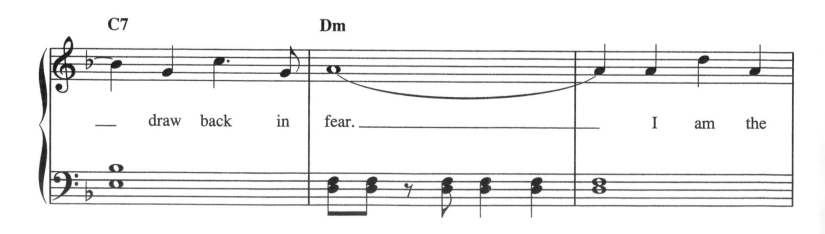

_____ draw back in fear. _____ I am the

mask you wear,___ it's me they hear.

{ Your / My } spi - rit and { my / your } voice ___ in one com-

bined; ___ the phan -

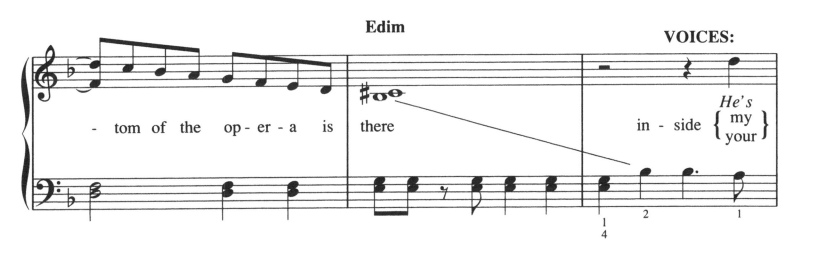

- tom of the op - er - a is there in - side { *He's* my / your }

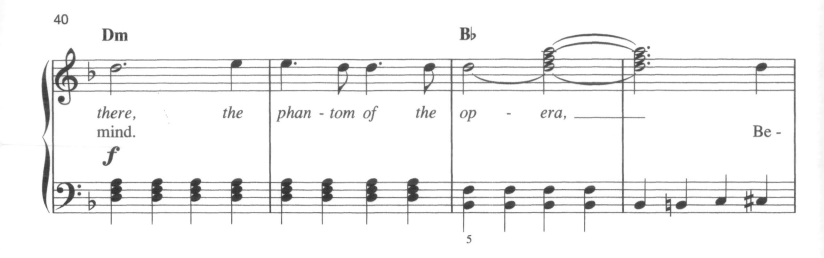

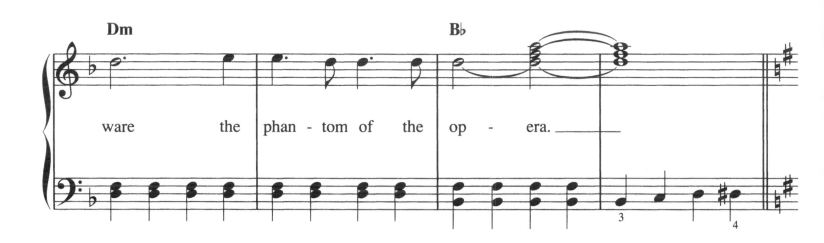

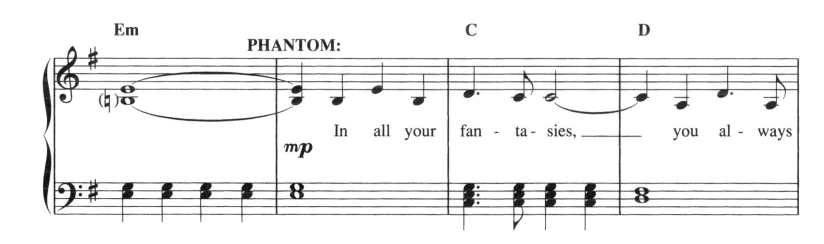

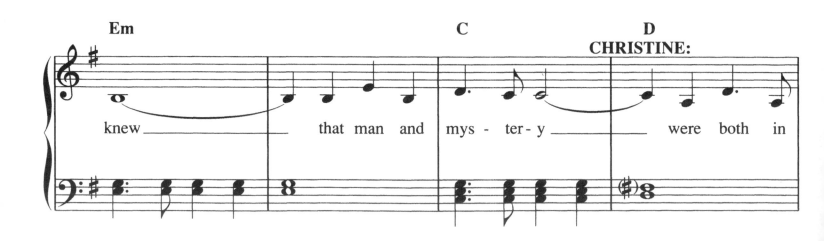

PHANTOM and CHRISTINE:

you._____ And in this la - by - rinth_____ where night is

blind,_____ the phan -

- tom of the op - er - a is {here/there}_____ in - side {my/your}

mind. **PHANTOM:** *(Spoken) Sing my angel of music!* **CHRISTINE:** He's

there the phan - tom of the op - era.

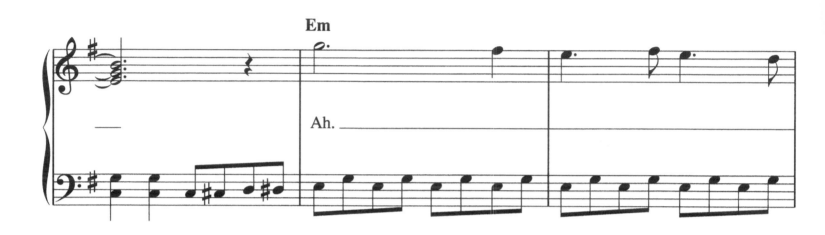

Ah.

PHANTOM:

CHRISTINE:

Sing, my angel, sing!

Ah!

PHANTOM:

Sing for me!

CHRISTINE:

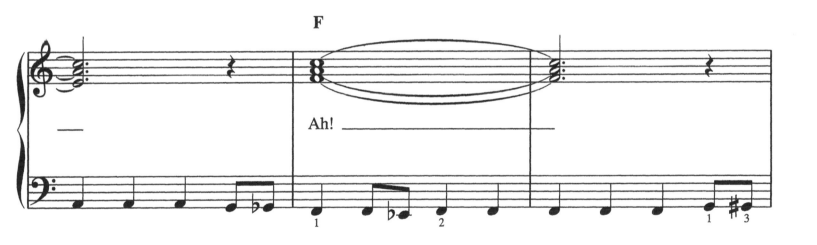

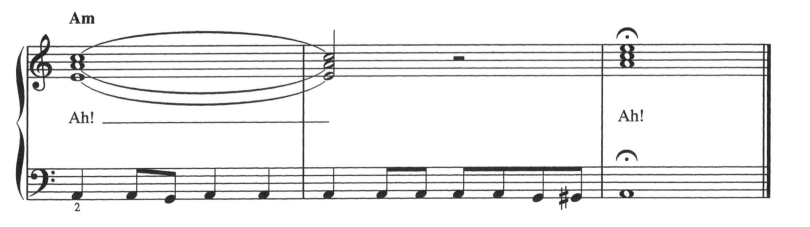

PIE JESU
(From "REQUIEM")

Music by ANDREW LLOYD WEBBER

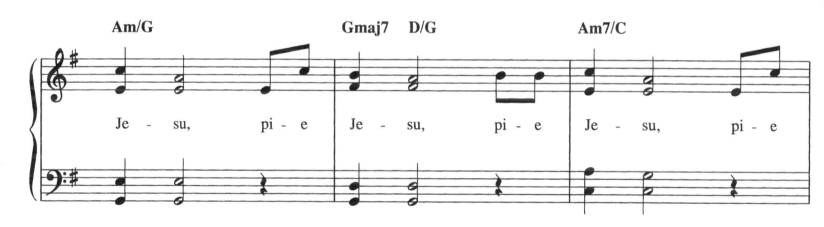

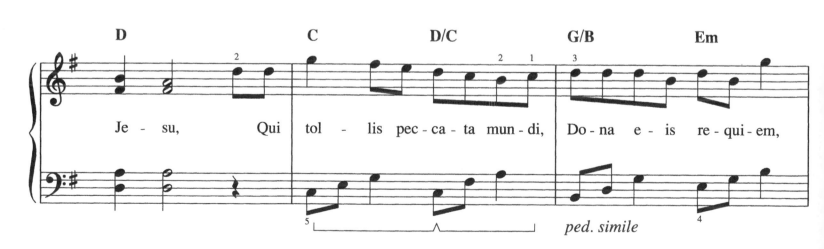

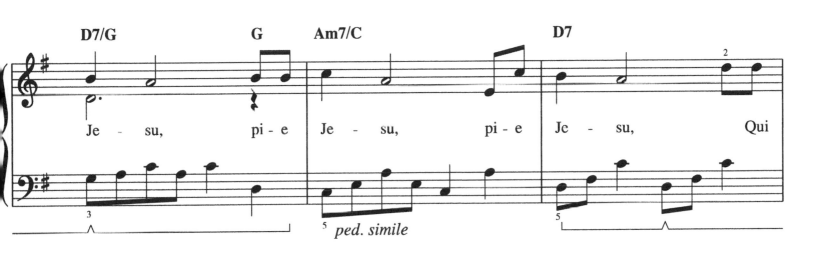

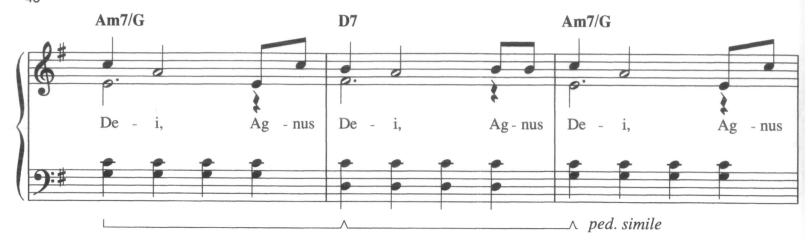

De - i, Ag - nus De - i, Ag - nus De - i, Ag - nus

ped. simile

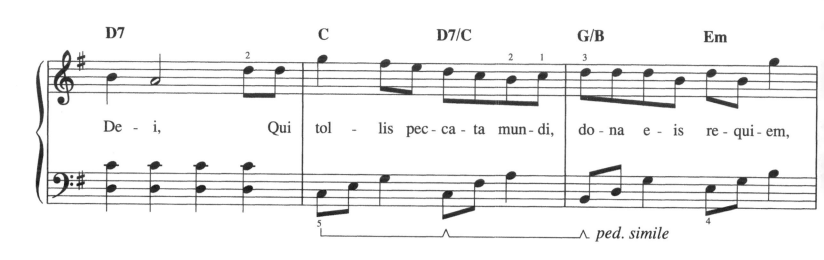

De - i, Qui tol - lis pec - ca - ta mun - di, do - na e - is re - qui - em,

ped. simile

do - na e - is re - qui - em. Sem - pi - ter - nam, sem - pi -

mp

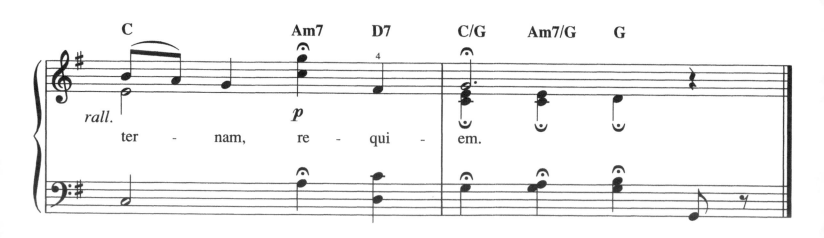

rall. ter - nam, re - qui - em.

p

SUPERSTAR
(From "JESUS CHRIST SUPERSTAR")

Lyric by TIM RICE
Music by ANDREW LLOYD WEBBER

Slowly

Moderate rock

Ev - 'ry time I look at you I don't un - der - stand, ___
Tell me what you think a - bout your friends at the top, ___

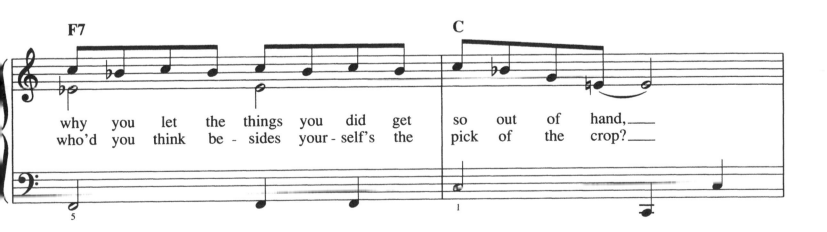

why you let the things you did get so out of hand, ___
who'd you think be - sides your - self's the pick of the crop? ___

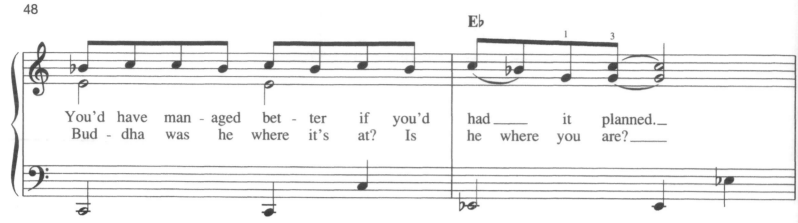

You'd have man - aged bet - ter if you'd had ____ it planned.__
Bud - dha was he where it's at? Is he where you are?___

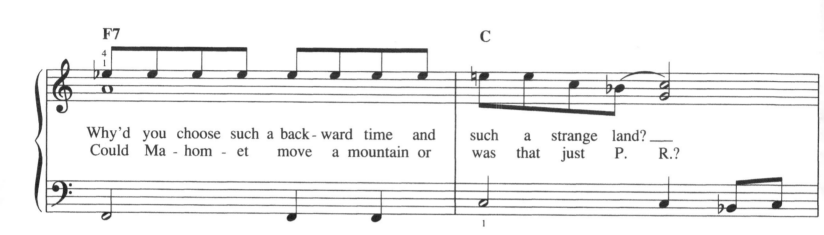

Why'd you choose such a back - ward time and such a strange land?___
Could Ma - hom - et move a mountain or was that just P. R.?

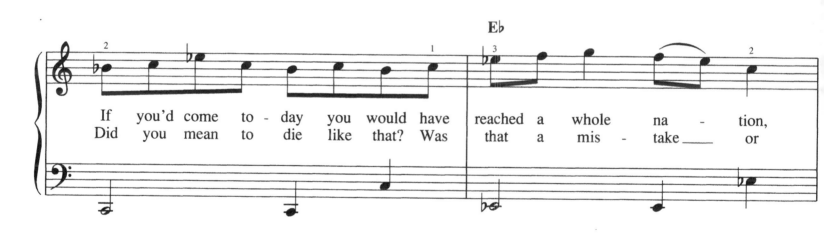

If you'd come to - day you would have reached a whole na - tion,
Did you mean to die like that? Was that a mis - take___ or

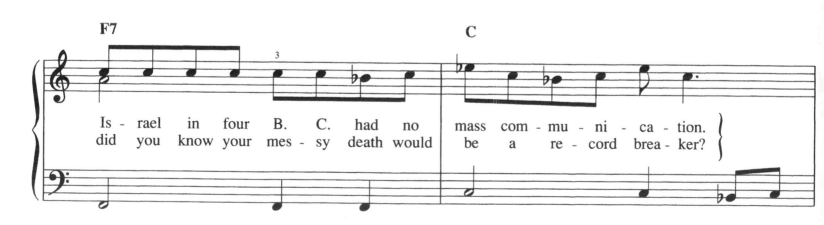

Is - rael in four B. C. had no mass com - mu - ni - ca - tion.
did you know your mes - sy death would be a re - cord brea - ker?

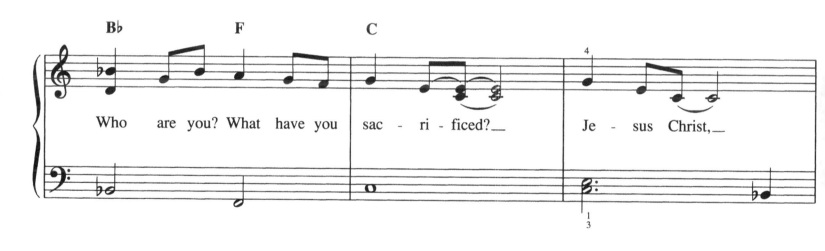

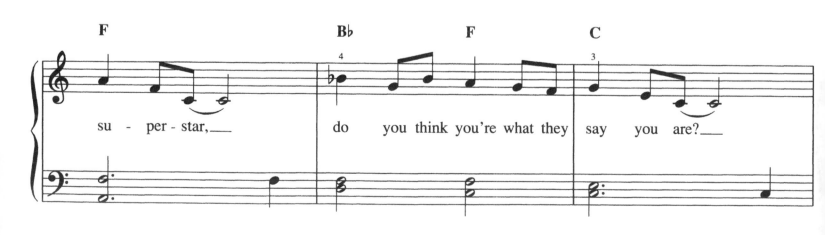

Je - sus Christ,___ su - per - star,___ do you think you're what they

say you are?___

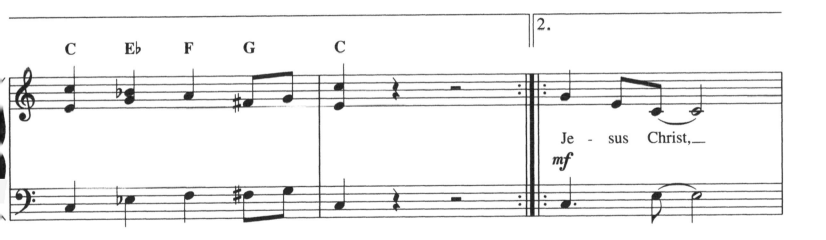

Je - sus Christ,___

mf

Repeat and fade

su - per - star,___ do you think you're what they say you are?___

TAKE THAT LOOK OFF YOUR FACE

(From "SONG AND DANCE")

Music by ANDREW LLOYD WEBBER
Lyrics by DON BLACK

Moderately

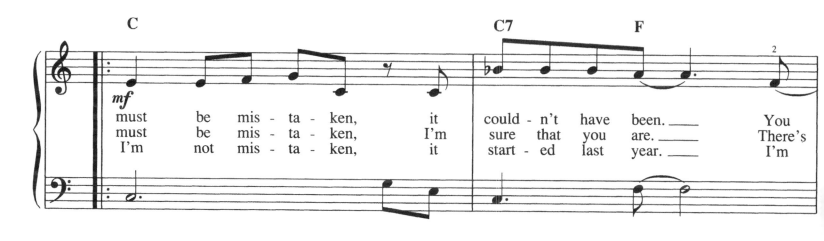

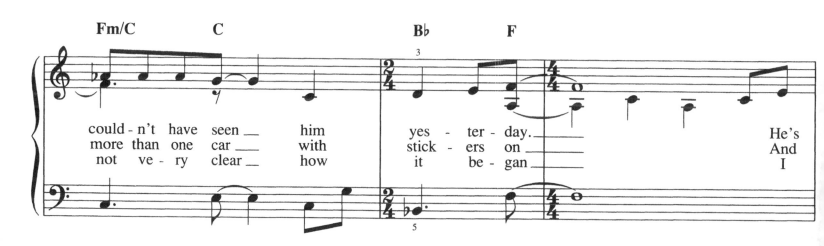

C/G **G** **Am**

do - ing some deal ___ up in Bal - ti - more now, ___ I
lots of young guys ___ wear cor - du - roy pants ___ and I'd
not - iced a change ___ but I just closed my eyes ___ As

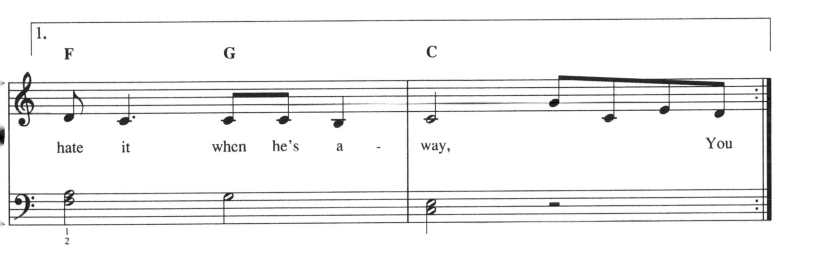

1.

F **G** **C**

hate it when he's a - way, You

2., 3.

F **G** **C** *Chorus*

know if he had - n't gone. *f* Take that
only a wo - man can. No I

C *(backing vocals)*

look off your face ___ (Take that look off your face ___) I can
did - n't dig deep ___ (No I did - n't dig deep ___) I did

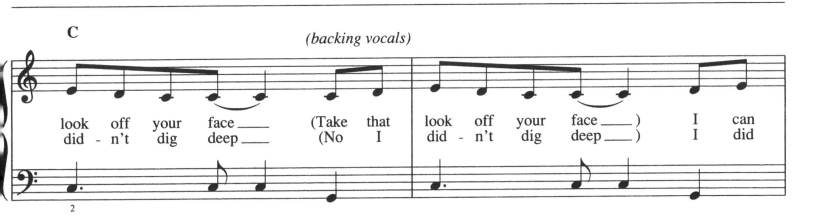

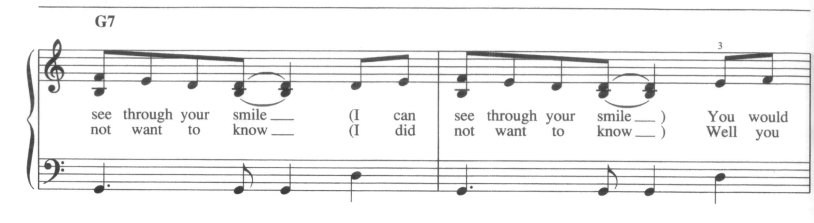

Second time to next strain *

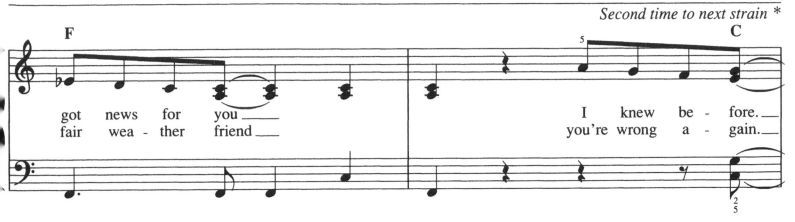

got news for you _____ I knew be - fore. _____
fair wea - ther friend _____ you're wrong a - gain. _____

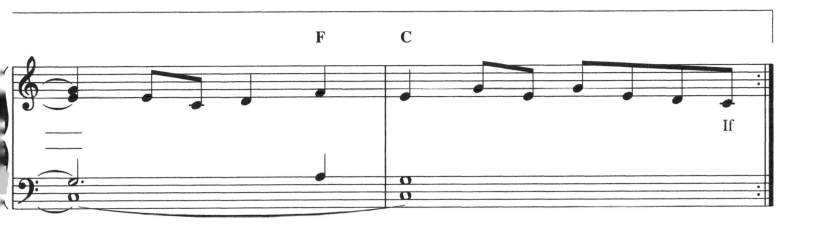

If

* *Next strain*

(Take that

look off your face _____) take that look off your face _____ (I can

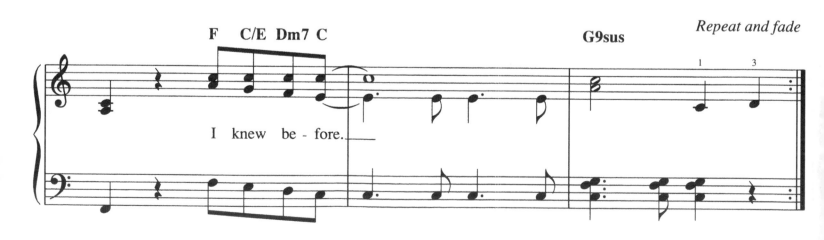

THINK OF ME
(From "THE PHANTOM OF THE OPERA")

Music by ANDREW LLOYD WEBBER
Lyrics by CHARLES HART
Additional Lyrics by RICHARD STILGOE

Moderately

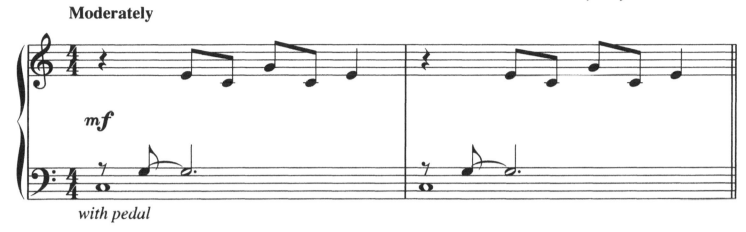

with pedal

CHRISTINE:

Think of me, think of me fond - ly when we've said good -

bye. Re - mem-ber me ev - 'ry so of - ten

58

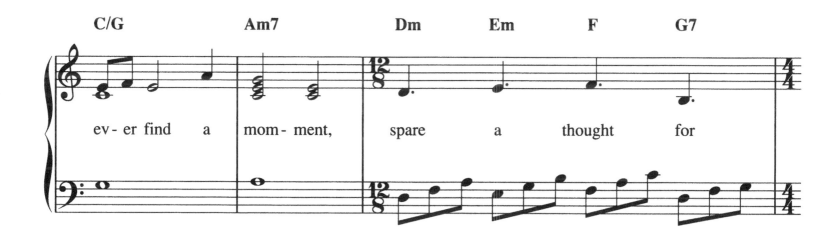

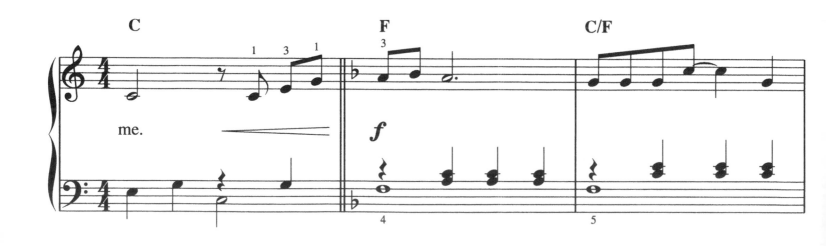

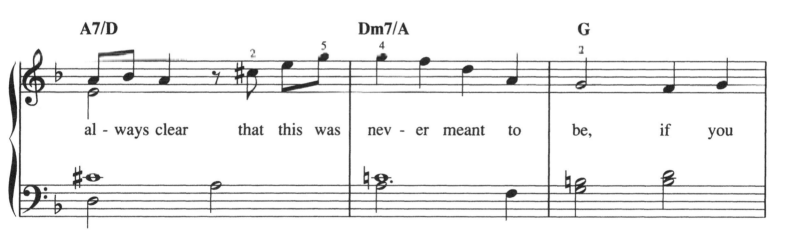

And though it's clear_____ though it was

al - ways clear   that this was   nev - er meant to   be,   if   you

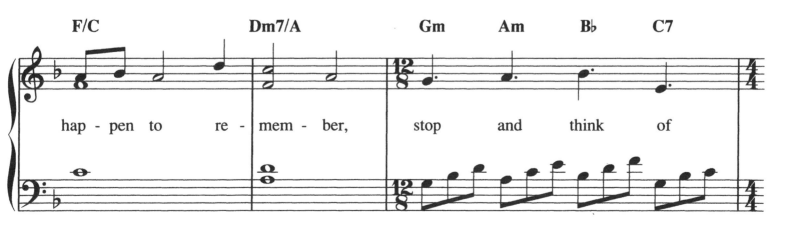

hap - pen to   re - mem - ber,   stop   and   think   of

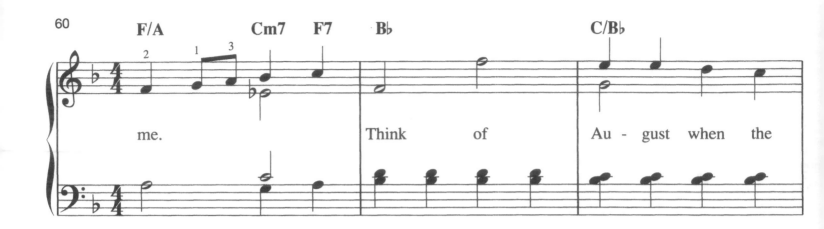

me. Think of Au - gust when the

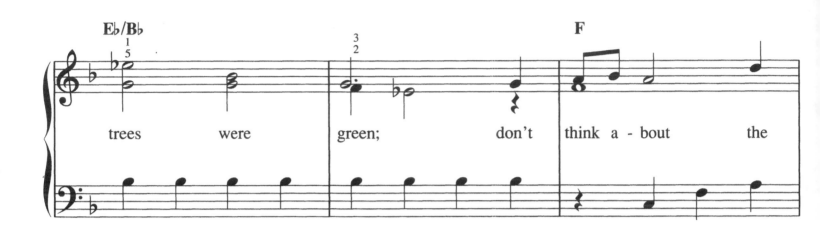

trees were green; don't think a - bout the

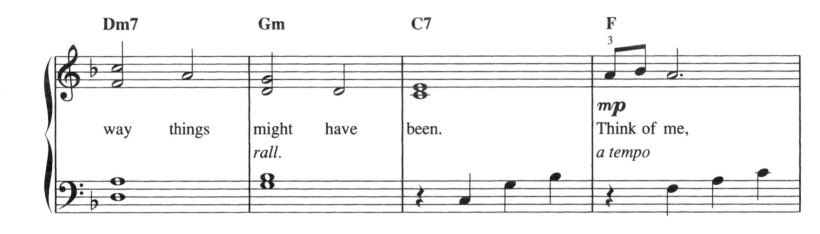

way things might have been. Think of me,
rall. *a tempo*

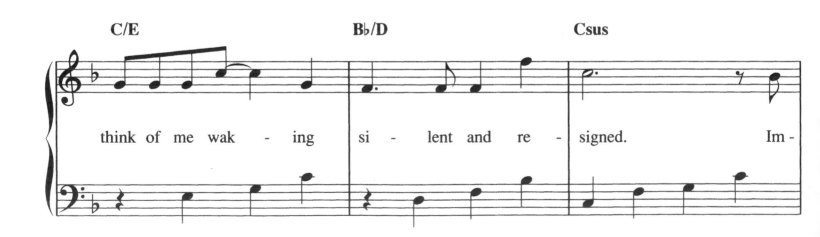

think of me wak - ing si - lent and re - signed. Im -

ag - ine me, try - ing too hard __ to put you from my

mind. Think of me __ please say you'll think of me what - ev - er

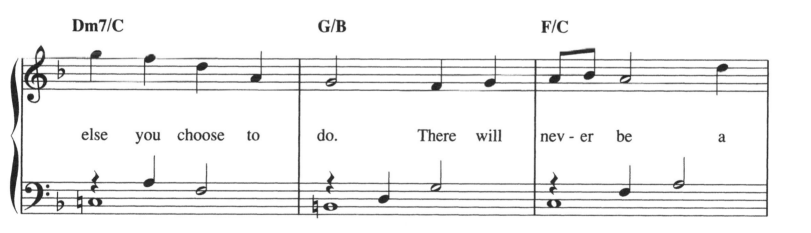

else you choose to do. There will nev - er be a

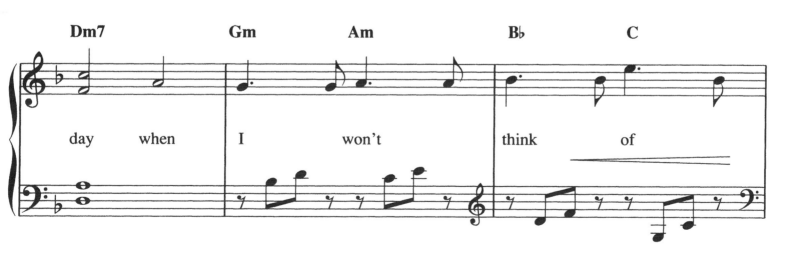

day when I won't think of

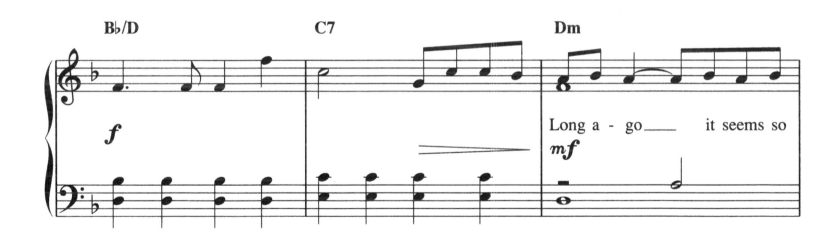

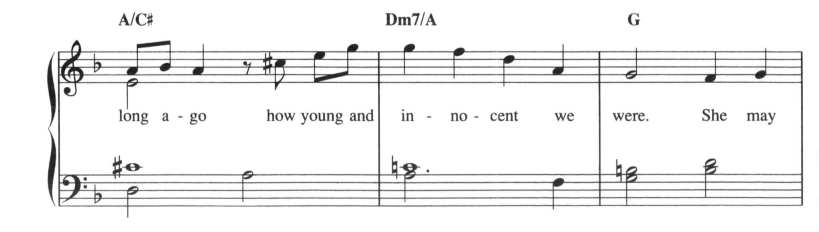

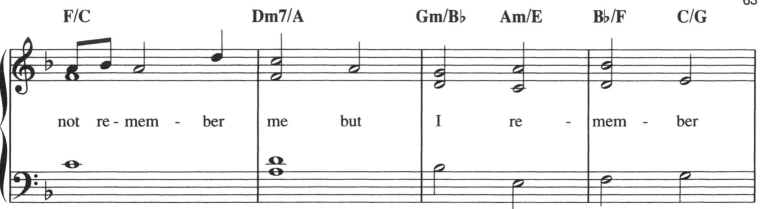

not re-mem - ber me but I re - mem - ber

CHRISTINE:

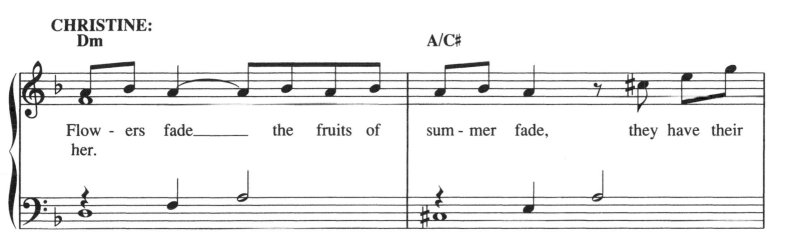

Flow - ers fade_____ the fruits of sum - mer fade, they have their
her.

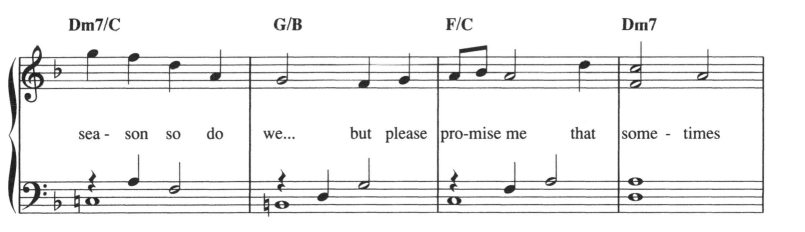

sea - son so do we... but please pro-mise me that some - times

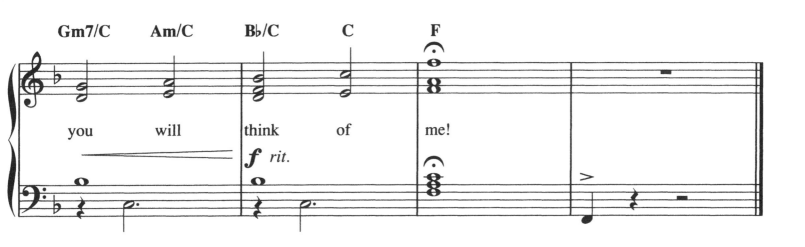

you will think of me!